30 Days of Grace

Prayers For Before Meals

Compiled By

Carla Shives

FirestormEditions

30 Days of Grace

Published by Firestorm Editions

Cover Art and Illustrations Provided For Commercial Use By

Clker-Free-Vector-Images from Pixabay

Gordon Johnson from Pixabay

OpenClipart-Vectors from Pixabay

First Printing: MAY, 2020

Printed in the United States of America

To My Children

Every time you eat and every time you drink,
remember Him.

INTRODUCTION

Imagine the family dinner table and a Norman Rockwell scene may spring to mind: platters of meat and vegetables, smiling children, and Mom serving up some potatoes as Dad carves the roast beef. And while that may seem to be the ideal, it's far from reality for most modern families.

A meal for today's family might look like take-out Chinese cartons, reheated leftovers, frozen lasagna, or pizza delivery. We might sit around a dining room table or gather at the kitchen island. And rather than a leisurely time of fellowship, it might be gobbled down in haste to ensure the kids get to soccer practice or ballet class.

In our family, as our children grew older, our meals became more disjointed. Busy lives meant tight schedules, and we started rushing through dinner to move on to our next event. Although we always said a blessing over our food before eating, it had become rote and meaningless, without true heart behind it. We were starting to repeat the same types of verses over and over again, which lead to everyone "zoning out" on the meaning of the words. I felt my family was missing the point of grace before meals, and it became evident when they complained about the food I prepared rather than appreciating God's provision.

It was time to bring gratitude back to our table, and I thought a good starting place would be to learn some new prayers for before our meals.

ABOUT THESE PRAYERS AND TALKING TOPICS

These prayers have been compiled from a variety of free and public sources, including traditional blessings that have been verbally passed down for generations, public domain books, and the Bible. When possible, I've credited the original source.

I've also included Talking Topics for you to use to nurture discussion during your meal time. Every family is different, and as you work your way through this book you may also come up with your own favorite topics for conversation. I encourage you to jot them down in the book so that you can revisit them in the future. A question like, "If you could create one law, what would it be?" might be answered differently by the same person just a few months later, and it is a wonderful experience to see how our children grow and mature in their responses.

HOW TO USE THIS BOOK

You don't need a Norman Rockwell meal to use this

book. It doesn't have to be opened only at dinner as the family sits in the formal dining room with a roast chicken, mashed potatoes, and braised carrots on the table. If breakfast is your family meal of the day, then choose a grace from this book as you eat your cereal together. These prayers can be used to bless everything from PB&J sandwiches to spaghetti to sushi. Don't feel tied to the traditional idea of an evening meal as the "family dinner." Since every meal is a time for thanking God for all that He has provided, this book can be used any time you're ready to eat. And if your family doesn't have time to eat together every single day, don't let that dissuade you! Even if you have only a few meals a week when your family gathers together, those moments of gratitude and discussion will help strengthen your relationship with God and with each other.

Each page of this book contains one prayer and three Talking Topics. I encourage you to use this book as it best works for your family, but one way is to choose a grace to read before the meal and then choose one Talking Topic from the same page. You may decide to go through this book in order, starting with the first prayer as you work your way toward the end. Or you may choose to just pick the blessing that most speaks to you that particular day. However you decide to use this book, I pray that it blesses your family and enriches your meals.

1

God is great! God is good!
Let us thank Him for our food.
By His hands we all are fed,
Thank you, Lord, for our daily bread.

TALKING TOPICS

➢ What is one way God blessed you today?
➢ What's your favorite memory from a family vacation?
➢ If you could own a restaurant, what type of food would you serve?

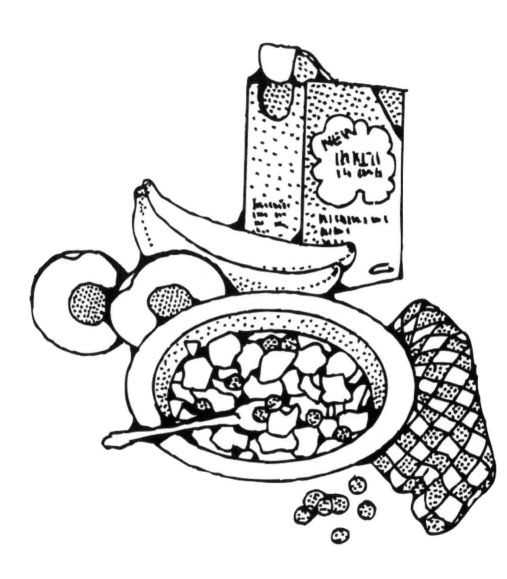

2

Dear Lord, thank You for this food.
Bless the hands that prepared it.
Bless it to our use and us to Your service,
And make us ever mindful of the needs
of others.

TALKING TOPICS

➢ How can we show God our thankfulness?
➢ If you could be any animal, what animal would you be?
➢ What qualities do you think make a good friend?

3

Father, we thank You for this food,
For health and strength and all things good.
May others all these blessings share,
And hearts be grateful everywhere.

TALKING TOPICS

➢ What happened today that made you feel glad?

➢ How can we show gratitude to family and friends?

➢ What's your favorite sweet treat and why?

4

Great God, Thou Giver of all good,
Accept our praise and bless our food.
Grace, health, and strength to us afford
Through Jesus Christ, our blessed Lord.

TALKING TOPICS

➤ How do you show others that you love them?

➤ What is your least favorite chore?

➤ What is your favorite flavor of ice cream?

5

Jesus, bless what Thou hast given,
Feed our souls with bread from heaven;
Guide and lead us all the way
In all that we may do and say.

TALKING TOPICS

➢ Did you encounter a difficult situation today when you needed God's help?

➢ Describe the perfect day.

➢ If you could create one law, what would it be?

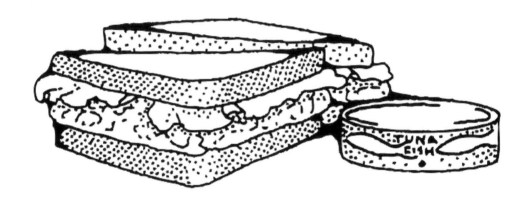

6

Bless us, oh Lord, and these Thy gifts,
Which we are about to receive
Through Thy bounty, through Christ
our Lord.

TALKING TOPICS

➤ If you could do today over again, what would you do differently?

➤ What makes you feel close to God?

➤ If you could choose a nickname for yourself, what would you choose?

7

Without Your sunshine and Your rain,
We would not have the golden grain.
Without Your love we'd not be fed.
We thank You, Lord, for our daily bread.

TALKING TOPICS

➤ If you could make tomorrow's dinner, what would you serve?

➤ What's a way you can bless someone you love?

➤ What is your least favorite thing that happened today?

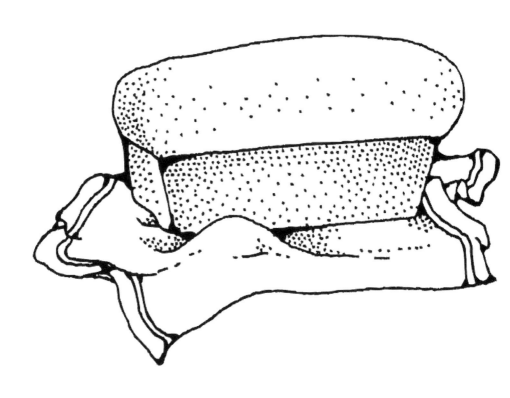

8

For each new morning with its light,
For rest and shelter of the night,
For health and food, for love and friends
For everything Thy goodness sends.

Ralph Waldo Emerson

TALKING TOPICS

➢ If you grew a garden, what would you most want to plant in it?

➢ What is your biggest fear?

➢ What is your favorite Bible story?

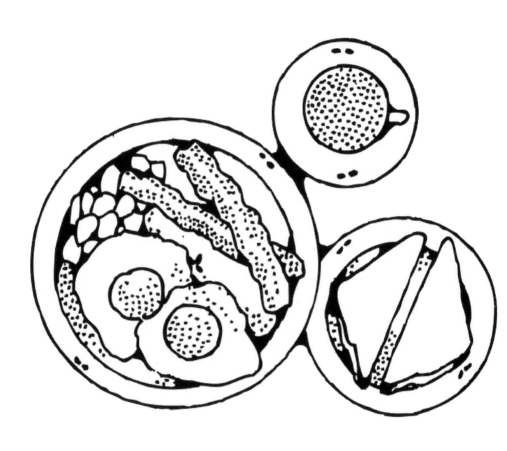

9

Oh, the Lord's been good to me,
And so I thank the Lord
For giving me the things I need:
The sun and the rain and the apple seed.
The Lord's been good to me.

Johnny Appleseed Grace

TALKING TOPICS

➤ Say something kind about each person here.

➤ What do you think heaven is like?

➤ What's one skill you'd like to learn?

10

Be present at our table, Lord:
Be here and everywhere adored.
Thy creatures bless, and grant that we
May feast in paradise with Thee.

John Cennick

TALKING TOPICS

➤ If you could switch places with someone else for one day, who would it be?

➤ What is one thing you learned today?

➤ What type of music makes you feel like singing?

11

Let them thank the Lord for His steadfast love,
for His wondrous works to the children of man!
For He satisfies the longing soul,
and the hungry soul He fills with good things.

Psalm 107:8-9

TALKING TOPICS

➢ How would you spend a million dollars?

➢ What do you think is your greatest talent?

➢ What historical figure do you admire most
and why?

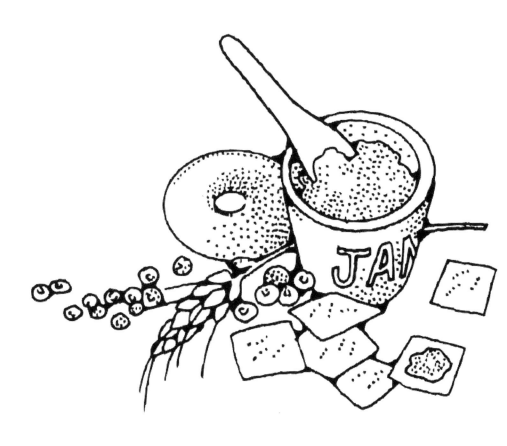

12

Come, Lord Jesus, be our guest,
and may our meal by you be blest.
And may there be a godly share,
On every table everywhere.

Martin Luther

TALKING TOPICS

➤ How can we pray for family or friends in need?
➤ Which friend would you like to invite over for dinner and why?
➤ What is your favorite movie and why?

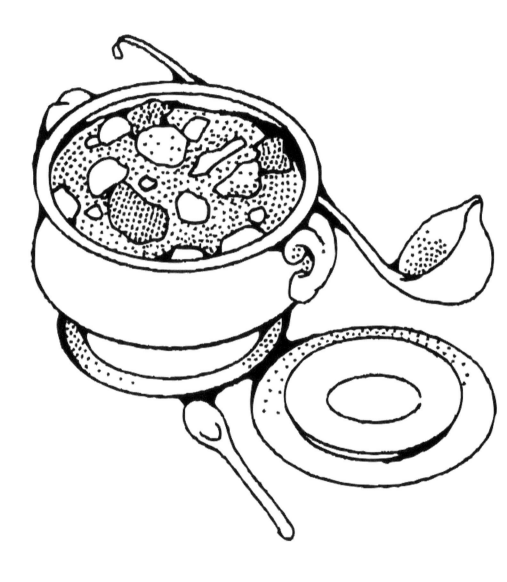

13

Lord, thank You for the food before us,
the family and friends beside us,
and the love between us.

TALKING TOPICS

➤ What happened today that made you feel mad?

➤ If you were alone on a deserted island, what three items would you want with you?

➤ What's the best compliment you've received?

CEREAL

14

Thank you, God, for this food,
For rest and home and all things good,
For wind and rain and sun above,
But most of all for those we love.

TALKING TOPICS

➢ If you and a friend have a disagreement, how would you handle it?

➢ What is your favorite game and why?

➢ What is your best birthday memory?

15

We thank you, God, for this our food,
For life and health and every good.
Let manna to our souls be given:
The bread of life sent down from heaven.

John Cennick

TALKING TOPICS

➤ What would you do if you were President of the country?

➤ What do you think it was like on Noah's ark?

➤ What do you think the future will be like?

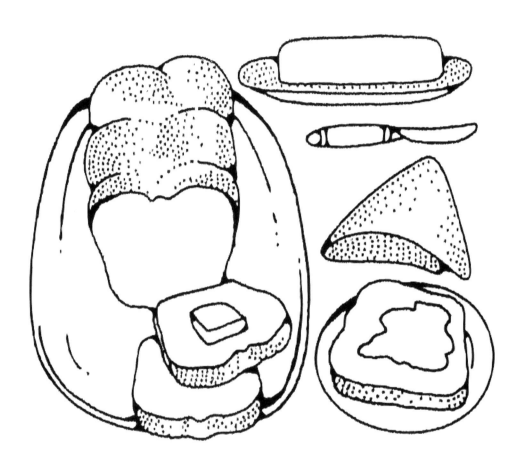

16

Lord Jesus, be our holy guest;
Our morning joy, our evening rest;
And with our daily bread impart,
Your love and peace to every heart.

TALKING TOPICS

➤ What famous person would you like to meet and why?

➤ If you had to give all your toys away except for one, which one would you keep?

➤ What is your favorite Bible story?

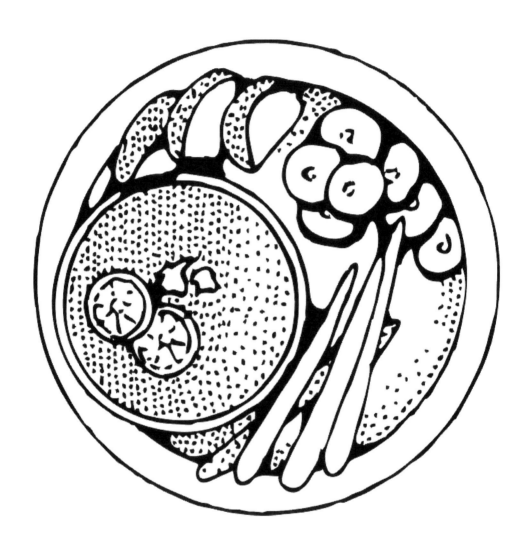

17

O thou who kindly dost provide For every
creature's want!
We bless Thee, God of Nature wide, For all
Thy goodness lent:
And if it please Thee, Heavenly Guide, May
never worse be sent;
But, whether granted, or denied, Lord, bless
us with content. Amen!

Robert Burns

TALKING TOPICS

➤ What are your favorite taco toppings?
➤ How can you be kind to an unhappy friend?
➤ What is your favorite thing that happened today?

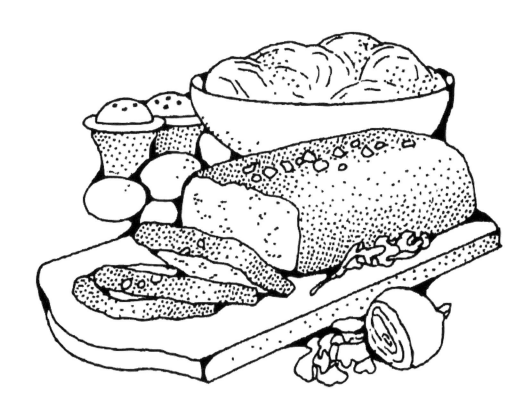

18

Great God, Thou Giver of all good,
Accept our praise and bless our food.
Grace, health, and strength to us afford
Through Jesus Christ, our blessed Lord.

TALKING TOPICS

➤ If you could outlaw one vegetable, which one would you choose?

➤ What do you want to be when you grow up?

➤ How do you like people to show their love for you?

19

For good food and those who prepare it,
For good friends with whom to share it,
We thank you, Lord.

TALKING TOPICS

➢ Name an animal that would make an interesting pet.

➢ If you could invent something to make the world a better place, what would it be?

➢ What is something you really love about God's creation?

20

We thank You Lord, for all you give;
the food we eat, the lives we live;
and to our loved ones far away,
please send your blessings, Lord, we pray.
And help us all to live our days
with thankful hearts and loving ways.

TALKING TOPICS

➤ What do you love about yourself?

➤ If you could only eat one food for the rest of your life, what would you choose?

➤ What is your favorite time of the day and why?

21

A thousand gifts thou does impart.
One more I ask, O Lord: A grateful heart.

George Herbert

TALKING TOPICS

➤ What happened today that made you feel sad?

➤ If you were at a party and you didn't know a single person, how would you feel?

➤ How did you see God working in your life today?

22

For food and health and happy days
Receive our gratitude and praise.
In serving others, Lord, may we
Repay our debt of love to thee.

TALKING TOPICS

➢ Describe what life would be like if you lived in a tropical jungle.

➢ Would you rather dance in the rain, snow, or sunshine?

➢ What are some ways we can show love to our enemies?

23

Rejoice always, pray without ceasing,
give thanks in all circumstances,
for this is the will of God in Christ Jesus
for you.

1 Thessalonians 5:18

TALKING TOPICS

➢ If you could make your own movie, what would it be about?

➢ Tell about a difficult time that God helped you through today.

➢ What is your favorite scent and why?

24

God our Father, Lord and Savior,
Thank You for Your love and favor.
Bless this food and drink we pray,
And all who shares with us today.

TALKING TOPICS

➢ What is your favorite thing to learn about?

➢ Would you rather travel by plane, train, boat, or automobile?

➢ If you could change one thing about your family, what would it be?

25

Be present at our table, Lord.
Be here and everywhere adored.
Thy creatures bless and grant that we
may feast in paradise with Thee.

John Cennick

TALKING TOPICS

➢ What is one way you can talk to others about God?

➢ If you could spend a day doing anything you wanted, what would you do?

➢ What is your favorite song and why?

26

Come, Lord Jesus, our guest to be
And bless these gifts
Bestowed by Thee.
And bless our loved ones everywhere,
And keep them in Your loving care.

TALKING TOPICS

➤ If you could travel through time, which time would you want to visit?

➤ How would you like to help others when you grow up?

➤ What's your favorite book and why?

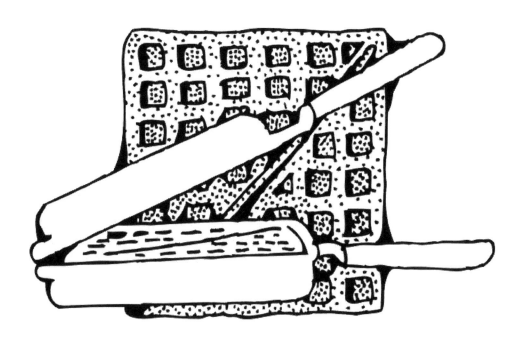

27

For food that stays our hunger,
For rest that brings us ease,
For homes where memories linger,
We give our thanks for these.

TALKING TOPICS

➤ What is your favorite article of clothing?

➤ Tell about one way you obeyed God today.

➤ If you could have a superpower, which superpower would you want?

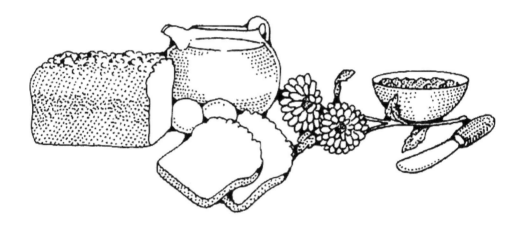

28

Praise God from Whom all blessings flow.
Praise Him all creatures here below.
Praise Him above ye heavenly hosts.
Praise Father, Son, and Holy Ghost.

TALKING TOPICS

➤ What is your favorite season and why?
➤ If you could meet someone from the past, who would it be?
➤ Describe the perfect vacation.

29

Our Heavenly Father, kind and good,
We thank Thee for our daily food.
We thank Thee for Thy love and care.
Be with us Lord, and hear our prayer.

TALKING TOPICS

➤ What is the best thing about being a kid?
➤ If you could travel anywhere in the world, where would you go?
➤ Which insect do you think is the creepiest?

30

In a world where so many are hungry,
May we eat this food with humble hearts.
In a world where so many are lonely,
May we share this friendship with joyful
hearts.

TALKING TOPICS

➤ Is there someone you know who is especially in need of prayer today?

➤ What is the funniest joke you've ever heard?

➤ Describe the perfect meal.

About Carla Shives

Carla Shives is a Christian wife and homeschooling mother, and thus she fulfills all the roles those jobs incorporate: personal chef, taxi driver, teacher, psychologist, cheerleader, housekeeper, coach, valet, travel planner, life coach, professional organizer, dishwasher, nurse, tailor, record keeper, photographer, public relations expert, event coordinator, hairstylist, personal assistant, grounds maintenance worker, interior designer, and private investigator.

When she gets a spare moment, Carla tries to find time to brush her hair, don a shirt without a food stain, and mop up the sticky spot that's been on her floor for a week.

And sometimes, during those rare moments when the stars are aligned and the angels are smiling down from heaven, Carla actually writes a book or two.

www.carlashives.com

Printed in Great Britain
by Amazon